OFFICIALLY RETIRED

QUOTES AND
QUIPS TO CELEBRATE
YOUR FREEDOM

OFFICIALLY RETIRED

Compiled by Paolo Ferrari

An Hachette UK Company
www.hachette.co.uk

Summersdale Publishers Ltd
Part of Octopus Publishing Group Limited
Carmelite House
50 Victoria Embankment
LONDON
EC4Y 0DZ
UK

www.summersdale.com

Printed and bound in China

ISBN: 978-1-83799-212-6

Substantial discounts on bulk quantities of Summersdale books are available to corporations, professional associations and other organizations. For details contact general enquiries: telephone: +44 (0) 1243 771107 or email: enquiries@summersdale.com.

TO...............................

FROM..........................

THERE'S ONE THING I ALWAYS WANTED TO DO BEFORE I QUIT... RETIRE!

Groucho Marx

A RETIRED HUSBAND IS OFTEN A WIFE'S FULL-TIME JOB.

Ella Harris

PROCRASTINATION
HAS ITS GOOD
SIDE, AS YOU
ALWAYS HAVE
SOMETHING TO
DO TOMORROW.

Milton Berle

Laughter helps
you live longer, but
so do antibiotics
and painkillers

THE MORE THINGS YOU DO, THE MORE YOU CAN DO.

Lucille Ball

FIND YOUR COMFORT ZONE

For many, retirement is the
time to start living life on the
edge – of a sofa or futon

THE
LONGER
I LIVE,
THE MORE
BEAUTIFUL
LIFE
BECOMES.

Frank Lloyd Wright

THE FUTURE BELONGS TO THOSE WHO BELIEVE IN THE BEAUTY OF THEIR DREAMS.

Eleanor Roosevelt

YOU MAY NOW
LEAVE DOUBTS
AND FEARS AT
HOME, BUT NOT
YOUR TEETH

KEEP
MOVING:
IT'S HARD
FOR OLD
AGE TO HIT
A MOVING
TARGET.

Joan Rivers

You know what's great about work? Nothing!

WHAT DO GARDENERS DO WHEN THEY RETIRE?

Bob Monkhouse

HELLO,
NEW YOU

Now that you're walking
a new path, take it easy
and wear comfy shoes

MY IDEA
OF A GOOD
WORKOUT
IS TWO
HOURS SPENT
WORRYING
ABOUT THE
BAGS UNDER
MY EYES.

Maureen Lipman

LET'S START A NEW TOMORROW, TODAY.

Neil Gaiman

IF YOU DON'T HAVE WRINKLES, YOU HAVEN'T LAUGHED ENOUGH.

Phyllis Diller

THERE ARE
WORSE THINGS
IN LIFE THAN
THE NINE-TO-
FIVE GRIND...
BUT NOT
VERY MANY

YOU'RE ONLY GIVEN A LITTLE SPARK OF MADNESS. YOU MUSTN'T LOSE IT.

Robin Williams

You can finally go
and visit long-lost
friends – assuming
they're all still alive

RETIREMENT:
IT'S NICE TO
GET OUT OF
THE RAT RACE,
BUT YOU HAVE
TO LEARN TO
GET ALONG
WITH LESS
CHEESE.

Gene Perret

SLOW DOWN

Whether you're learning
new skills or gaining
new knowledge, taking
things easy should be
your prerogative

I'M HAPPY TO REPORT THAT MY INNER CHILD IS STILL AGELESS.

James Broughton

HOW
SIMPLE LIFE
BECOMES
WHEN
THINGS LIKE
MIRRORS ARE
FORGOTTEN.

Daphne du Maurier

RETIREMENT
IS WHEN YOU
REALIZE YOU
WERE BORN
TO GO WILD,
BUT ONLY
UNTIL 9 P.M.

NONE ARE SO OLD AS THOSE WHO HAVE OUTLIVED ENTHUSIASM.

Henry David Thoreau

Scientists say that
dining al fresco lowers
stress and anxiety while
increasing envy among
those stuck at work

WHEN
SOME PEOPLE
RETIRE,
IT'S GOING
TO BE MIGHTY
HARD TO
BE ABLE TO
TELL THE
DIFFERENCE.

Virginia Graham

THE RETIREMENT COMMANDMENT

Thou shall not speak the word "work" again except to wind someone up

YOU CAN'T HELP GETTING OLDER, BUT YOU DON'T HAVE TO GET OLD.

George Burns

GETTING
OLD IS LIKE
CLIMBING A
MOUNTAIN;
YOU GET
A LITTLE OUT
OF BREATH,
BUT THE
VIEW IS MUCH
BETTER!

Ingrid Bergman

RETIREMENT CAN TRIGGER ODD COMPULSIONS SUCH AS PUTTING UP SHELVES, REMOVING SKIRTING BOARDS AND OTHER DIY PROJECTS YOU TOTALLY SUCK AT

I HAVE THE
BODY OF AN
18-YEAR-OLD.
I KEEP IT IN
THE FRIDGE.

Spike Milligan

No one is
an island – until
they retire to
the Caribbean

SOME OF
THE BEST
MEMORIES
ARE MADE IN
FLIP-FLOPS.

Kellie Elmore

KNOWLEDGE IS POWER

With a doctorate in
leisure, you'll soon be
asked for advice. Be sure
to charge accordingly.

WORKING PEOPLE HAVE A LOT OF BAD HABITS, BUT THE WORST OF THESE IS WORK.

Clarence Darrow

IT'S
BETTER BEING
COMPLETELY
RIDICULOUS
THAN
UNBELIEVABLY
BORING.

Marilyn Monroe

LAUGHTER MAY BE THE BEST MEDICINE, BUT A JOKE IS NO SUBSTITUTE FOR A HIP REPLACEMENT

I DON'T FEEL OLD.
I DON'T FEEL
ANYTHING TILL NOON.
THAT'S WHEN IT'S
TIME FOR MY NAP.

Bob Hope

Retirement is the
pathway to happiness,
but alcohol will get
you there faster

I HAVEN'T BEEN EVERYWHERE, BUT IT'S ON MY LIST.

Susan Sontag

BE YOURSELF

Be brave, be bold and never follow in the footsteps of others, unless you're in an emergency evacuation

ENJOY PRESENT PLEASURES IN SUCH A WAY AS NOT TO INJURE FUTURE ONES.

Seneca

IF YOU
ALWAYS
DO WHAT
INTERESTS
YOU, AT
LEAST ONE
PERSON IS
PLEASED.

Katharine Hepburn

LIFE IS
LIKE GOOD
WHISKY — IT
IMPROVES
WITH AGE

THERE'S NEVER ENOUGH TIME TO DO ALL THE NOTHING YOU WANT.

Bill Watterson

Clocks may
go backwards
or forwards, but
the truth is...
who cares?

STAY YOUNG
AT HEART,
KIND IN SPIRIT,
AND ENJOY
RETIREMENT
LIVING.

Danielle Duckery

PETS

Buy a pet... they may
be the only ones willing
to listen to your tales

RETIREMENT ITSELF IS THE BEST GIFT. NO GOLD WATCH COULD EVER TOP IT.

Abigail Charleson

THE POSITIVE
THINKER SEES
THE INVISIBLE,
FEELS THE
INTANGIBLE
AND ACHIEVES
THE
IMPOSSIBLE.

Winston Churchill

RECURRING
CONUNDRUMS
WILL NOW BE:
GET TIPSY,
DRUNK OR
TOTALLY
WASTED?

YOU'RE RETIRED: GOODBYE TENSION, HELLO PENSION!

Anonymous

ONE MUST DARE TO BE HAPPY.

Gertrude Stein

IN RETIREMENT, I LOOK FOR DAYS OFF FROM MY DAYS OFF.

Mason Cooley

HAPPINESS

... is the ability to accept
a few simple truths:

1) You will never be 20 again

2) You will never date a celeb

3) It doesn't hurt to dream

MY FUTURE STARTS WHEN I WAKE UP EVERY MORNING.

Miles Davis

I'M AFRAID OF NOTHING EXCEPT BEING BORED!

Greta Garbo

AFTER RETIREMENT, "ANY PORT IN A STORM" ACTUALLY MEANS A GOOD WINE

I WISH I COULD
TELL YOU IT
GETS BETTER.
IT DOESN'T GET
BETTER... YOU
GET BETTER.

Joan Rivers

Well done! You made it!
From now on everything
just clicks into place,
including your dentures.

DON'T UNDERESTIMATE THE VALUE OF DOING NOTHING.

A. A. Milne

I BEG YOUR PARDON?

If you can't hear life
telling you to follow
your dreams, you might
need a hearing aid

I CAN'T
BELIEVE I'M
BREATHING
AND HAPPY
AND THRIVING.

Tig Notaro

RETIREMENT IS WHEN, EVERY YEAR, YOUR BLOOD PRESSURE GETS HIGHER AND YOUR BANK BALANCE GETS LOWER.

Bob Orben

WITH AGE
COMES WISDOM,
AND WITH
WISDOM COMES
THE ABILITY
TO BLAME
OTHERS FOR
YOUR MISTAKES

WHEN SOMEONE TELLS ME "NO", IT DOESN'T MEAN I CAN'T DO IT, IT SIMPLY MEANS I CAN'T DO IT WITH THEM.

Karen E. Quinones Miller

Commuting to
work is now a thing
of the past, like a
full head of hair

DON'T SIMPLY RETIRE FROM SOMETHING; HAVE SOMETHING TO RETIRE TO.

Harry Emerson Fosdick

BIRTHDAYS

Presents to ask for after you retire: garden-centre vouchers and books in large print

THE
BODY DOES
WHATEVER
IT WANTS.
I AM NOT
MY BODY;
I AM MY
MIND.

Rita Levi-Montalcini

ENTHUSIASM IS EVERYTHING. IT MUST BE TAUT AND VIBRATING LIKE A GUITAR STRING.

Pelé

THINGS YOU WILL
NOW NEVER DO
INCLUDE: GOING TO
WORK, FANCYING
SOMEONE OLDER
AND BEING
THE NEW FACE
OF L'ORÉAL

IF YOU OBEY ALL THE RULES, YOU MISS ALL THE FUN.

Katharine Hepburn

You know what?
You are nowhere
near as old as you
think when viewed
from a distance.

HIS DOCTOR
TOLD HIM TO PLAY
36 HOLES A DAY,
SO HE WENT OUT
AND BOUGHT
A HARMONICA.

Milton Berle

NEVER DRINK
BLACK COFFEE
AT LUNCH; IT
WILL KEEP YOU
AWAKE ALL
AFTERNOON.

Jilly Cooper

RETIREMENT MEANS NO PRESSURE, NO STRESS, NO HEARTACHE... UNLESS YOU PLAY GOLF.

Gene Perret

RETIREMENT
IS THE PERIOD
IN LIFE WHEN
YOU STOP
QUOTING THE
PROVERB THAT
TIME IS MONEY.

Evan Esar

THE TROUBLE WITH RETIREMENT IS THAT IT IS EASY TO GO DOWN MEMORY LANE BUT HARD TO COME BACK UP

I OWN NOTHING
OF VALUE AT ALL.
I SPEND MONEY
ON EXPERIENCES.

Miranda Hart

Retiring is easy,
but retiring with
your original teeth
and hair is a real
accomplishment

CHANCE IS
THE ONLY
SOURCE
OF TRUE
NOVELTY.

Francis Crick

EASY DOES IT

Retirement and alcohol
go hand in hand...
be moderate in all things
except moderation

SEEING TWILIGHT FALL SHOULD BE PRESCRIBED BY DOCTORS.

Marlene Dietrich

ONLY THOSE
WHO WILL
RISK GOING
TOO FAR CAN
POSSIBLY FIND
OUT HOW FAR
ONE CAN GO.

T. S. Eliot

THE DRESS CODE FOR RETIREMENT IS "WHATEVER"

WHEN THE SUN COMES UP, I HAVE MORALS AGAIN.

Elayne Boosler

Now you're retired the
world is your oyster.
It's time for you to
find the pearls.

HALF OUR
LIFE IS SPENT
TRYING
TO FIND
SOMETHING
TO DO WITH
THE TIME WE
HAVE RUSHED
THROUGH
LIFE TRYING
TO SAVE.

Will Rogers

GET ORGANIZED

If you're having trouble staying organized, refer to your "to-do-whenever" list

LIFE IS A DARING ADVENTURE OR NOTHING AT ALL.

Helen Keller

I'M THANKFUL
FOR THE
THREE-OUNCE
ZIPLOC BAG SO
THAT I HAVE
SOMEWHERE
TO PUT MY
SAVINGS.

Paula Poundstone

FROM NOW
ON, THE ONLY
THING THAT
SEPARATES
BRUNCH FROM
LUNCH IS YOUR
HEARING

THE SOUL SHOULD
ALWAYS STAND
AJAR, READY
TO WELCOME
THE ECSTATIC
EXPERIENCE.

Emily Dickinson

There has never been
a better time to go after
your dreams, especially
now that senior travel
discounts are available

FOR MANY,
RETIREMENT
IS A TIME FOR
PERSONAL
GROWTH,
WHICH
BECOMES
THE PATH
TO GREATER
FREEDOM.

Robert Delamontagne

COFFEE O'CLOCK

As you age, go steady on coffee. It could impact your freedom of espresso.

AGEING SEEMS TO BE THE ONLY AVAILABLE WAY TO LIVE A LONG LIFE.

Kitty O'Neill Collins

LIFE IS A
JOURNEY.
HOW WE
TRAVEL IS
REALLY UP
TO US.

Paulo Coelho

WITH AGE
COMES
WISDOM... AND
QUITE OFTEN
AN EMPTY
WINE RACK

A GOOD TRAVELLER
HAS NO FIXED PLANS,
AND IS NOT INTENT
ON ARRIVING.

Lao Tzu

Retirement is a good
time to embrace new
activities, but at your
age, "happy hour" might
just be a long snooze

TO SUCCEED
IN LIFE,
YOU NEED
THREE THINGS:
A WISHBONE,
A BACKBONE
AND A
FUNNY BONE.

Reba McEntire

STAY HEALTHY

Dieting may be difficult in retirement, so the next time you fancy a pastry, consider jogging to the nearest shop

HOLD FAST TO DREAMS, FOR IF DREAMS DIE, LIFE IS A BROKEN-WINGED BIRD THAT CANNOT FLY.

Langston Hughes

HAVE THE
COURAGE TO
FOLLOW YOUR
HEART AND
INTUITION.
THEY SOMEHOW
ALREADY KNOW
WHAT YOU
TRULY WANT.

Steve Jobs

AT YOUR AGE,
IT'S IMPORTANT
TO NEVER TURN
YOUR BACK ON
YOUR FRIENDS,
ESPECIALLY
WHEN REVERSING

MEMORIES ARE LIKE MULLIGATAWNY SOUP IN A CHEAP RESTAURANT. IT IS BEST NOT TO STIR THEM.

P. G. Wodehouse

With age comes wisdom.
But who wants that?

THERE IS A WHOLE NEW KIND OF LIFE AHEAD, FULL OF EXPERIENCES JUST WAITING TO HAPPEN. SOME CALL IT RETIREMENT; I CALL IT BLISS.

Betty Sullivan

BE PREPARED

There are two things in life for which we're seldom prepared: hangovers and retirement. Make sure to stay hydrated and have a pension plan.

I LOVE FOOLS' EXPERIMENTS. I AM ALWAYS MAKING THEM.

Charles Darwin

WHEN
HUMOUR
GOES,
THERE GOES
CIVILIZATION.

Erma Bombeck

LIFE IS WHAT
HAPPENS TO
YOU WHILE
YOU'RE BUSY
DECIDING
BETWEEN A
LUXURY SPA OR
CITY BREAK

ALL I CAN SAY ABOUT LIFE IS "OH GOD, ENJOY IT!"

Bob Newhart

I'M THANKFUL
THAT MY
MEMORY IS
GOOD BECAUSE
MY VISION
IS GOING.

Paula Poundstone

YOU CAN'T EXPECT
TO HIT THE JACKPOT
IF YOU DON'T PUT
A FEW NICKELS
IN THE MACHINE.

Flip Wilson

GARDENING TIME

Roses are red,
violets are blue... but
if in doubt, visit your
nearest garden centre

IF THE PATH
BE BEAUTIFUL,
LET US NOT
ASK WHERE
IT LEADS.

Anatole France

IF YOU HAD YOUR LIFE TO LIVE OVER AGAIN, DO IT OVERSEAS.

Henny Youngman

I THINK
I'D MAKE A
PRETTY GOOD
PRESIDENT,
AND THEY
HAVE A GREAT
PENSION PLAN.

Pat Paulsen

LIFE BEGINS AT THE END OF YOUR COMFORT ZONE.

Neale Donald Walsch

With so many
things to do and
share, silence
becomes a thing to
look forward to

AGE IS
AN ISSUE OF
MIND OVER
MATTER.
IF YOU
DON'T MIND,
IT DOESN'T
MATTER.

Anonymous

SHARING
IS CARING

Nice things in life are
meant to be shared...
including the entire packet
of biscuits you just scoffed

IF I HAD TO LIVE
MY LIFE AGAIN,
I'D MAKE THE
SAME MISTAKES,
ONLY SOONER.

Tallulah Bankhead

GAINFULLY UNEMPLOYED, VERY PROUD OF IT, TOO.

Charles Baxter

RETIREMENT
IS PRICELESS
UNTIL YOU
GET BANK
STATEMENTS

LIFE ISN'T ABOUT FINDING YOURSELF. LIFE IS ABOUT CREATING YOURSELF.

George Bernard Shaw

You know you're
getting really good
at being retired when
even your dog can
no longer stand you

LAZINESS IS NOTHING MORE THAN THE HABIT OF RESTING BEFORE YOU GET TIRED.

Jules Renard

FAMILY

Watching your family grow
up will be fun, but you might
need a pair of bifocals

YOU MUST LOVE AND CARE FOR YOURSELF BECAUSE THAT'S WHEN THE BEST COMES OUT.

Tina Turner

WE DON'T
GROW OLDER;
WE GROW
RIPER.

Pablo Picasso

YOUR EYES
MIGHT STILL BE
PERFECT, BUT
REMEMBER,
EVERYTHING
ELSE MIGHT
GET BLURRY

DON'T ACT YOUR AGE IN RETIREMENT. ACT LIKE THE INNER YOUNG PERSON YOU HAVE ALWAYS BEEN.

J. A. West

Not only is weekday golf a must, but it's also now the law

PROCRASTINATION
IS THE ART OF
KEEPING UP WITH
YESTERDAY.

Don Marquis

INTERESTS & ACTIVITIES

As you get older you must prepare for fatigue, anxiety and muscle aches... and that's just when getting out of bed!

WHY WOULD I WORRY ABOUT GETTING OLDER – WHAT'S TO MOAN ABOUT?

Dawn French

GREAT IS
THE ART OF
BEGINNING –
GREATER IS
THE ART OF
RETIRING.

Anonymous

RETIREMENT IS WHEN YOU REALIZE THAT YOU DON'T HAVE TO BE MUSICAL TO BLOW YOUR OWN TRUMPET

I'VE TOLD SO MANY
LIES ABOUT MY AGE,
I DON'T KNOW HOW
OLD I AM MYSELF.

Ruby Wax

Take it slow; at your
age actions creak
louder than words

SPEAK LITTLE, DO MUCH.

Benjamin Franklin

FUN & FROLICS

Go easy on crosswords.
At your age they may
cause vowel irritation.

I DON'T PLAN TO GROW OLD GRACEFULLY. I PLAN TO HAVE FACELIFTS UNTIL MY EARS MEET.

Rita Rudner

IT'S NEVER TOO LATE – NEVER TOO LATE TO START OVER, NEVER TOO LATE TO BE HAPPY.

Jane Fonda

THE MOST DIFFICULT TIME IN A PERSON'S LIFE IS THE FIRST WEEK OF RETIREMENT; ALL THOSE HIGH-FIVES CAN BE REALLY PAINFUL!

THE ONLY FAILURE IS NOT KNOWING HOW TO BE HAPPY.

Celine Dion

Happy retirement. I said…
HAPPY RETIREMENT.

IF YOU'RE
GOING TO DO
SOMETHING
TONIGHT THAT
YOU'LL BE
SORRY FOR
TOMORROW
MORNING,
SLEEP LATE.

Henny Youngman

AGE IS SOMETHING THAT DOESN'T MATTER, UNLESS YOU ARE A CHEESE.

Luis Buñuel

THE RETIREMENT PUZZLE BOOK
Paperback
978-1-80007-839-0

This collection of verbal and visual challenges will help you stay sharp and stimulated as you embark on a new chapter in life. From quick-fire trivia questions to crosswords and sudoku, whether you're a recent retiree or have been enjoying your freedom for years, there's plenty in these pages to keep you busy and set your mind purring.

GROWING OLD DOESN'T MEAN GROWING UP

Mike Haskins and Clive Whichelow

Hardback

978-1-80007-403-3

So you're a little bit older. So what? Forget the creaking joints and fleeing follicles – this book is the perfect dose of inspiration and merriment for anyone with more than a few candles on their birthday cake.

Have you enjoyed this book?
If so, find us on Facebook at
Summersdale Publishers,
on Twitter at @Summersdale
and on Instagram and TikTok at
@summersdalebooks and get in
touch. We'd love to hear from you!

www.summersdale.com